THE
LONG
WEEKEND

THE LONG WEEKEND

RITA ANN
HIGGINS

GILL BOOKS

OTHER WORKS BY RITA ANN HIGGINS

POETRY
Goddess on the Mervue Bus (Salmon, 1986)
Witch in the Bushes (Salmon, 1988)
Goddess and Witch (Salmon, 1990)
Philomena's Revenge (Salmon, 1992)
Higher Purchase (Salmon, 1996)
Sunny Side Plucked (Bloodaxe, 1996)
An Awful Racket (Bloodaxe, 2001)
Throw in the Vowels: New & Selected Poems (Bloodaxe, 2005)
Ireland is Changing Mother (Bloodaxe, 2011)
Tongulish (Bloodaxe, 2016)
Pathogens Love a Patsy (Salmon, 2020)

ESSAYS & POEMS
Our Killer City (Salmon, 2019)

MEMOIR
Hurting God (Salmon, 2010)

PLAYS
Face Licker Come Home (Salmon, 1991)
God of the Hatch Man (1992)
Colie Lally Doesn't Live in a Bucket (1993)
Down All the Roundabouts (1999)
The Empty Frame (2008)
The Plastic Bag, for radio (2008)
The Colossal Longing of Julie Connors (2014)

SCREENPLAYS
The Big Break (2004)
Straois/The Smirk (2018)
Fracture (2024)

EDITOR
Out the Clara Road: The Offaly Anthology (1999)
Word and Image: a collection of poems from Sunderland Women's Centre and Washington Bridge Centre (2000)
FIZZ: Poetry of resistance and challenge, an anthology written by young people at risk, co-editor (2004)

In deeply poignant, intelligent and powerful poems, *The Long Weekend* spans a life lived with canny observation, lyricism and sharp wit. Higgins makes brilliant the banal, spins music from the mundane, and speaks truth to power in her celebration of the everyday lives we lead.

For decades she has been one of the most powerful and empathetic voices in writing, balancing despair with hope, love with loss and our internal landscapes with the beauty of the natural world.

The Long Weekend is a haunting, beautiful collection of poems that commands attention and bears witness to life's struggle. This collection confirms Higgins as one of our greatest poets.

– *Elaine Feeney, author of* How to Build a Boat

Rita Ann Higgins's *The Long Weekend* is a work of immense thoughtfulness – with a lightness of touch and a ludic mastery, Higgins reveals at a granular level the various idiosyncrasies of place and personhood. Silly, funny, and at times deeply discomfiting, these poems use vibrant and buoyant anecdote to invite you in, only to sadden and unsettle you with what might be hiding behind the linguistic misdirection.

– *Susannah Dickey, author of* Tennis Lessons *and* ISDAL

Gill Books
Hume Avenue
Park West
Dublin 12
www.gillbooks.ie

Gill Books is an imprint of M.H. Gill & Co.

© Rita Ann Higgins, 2024

978 1 8045 8066 0
Designed by Bartek Janczak
Proofread by Djinn van Noorden
Printed and bound in the UK using 100% renewable electricity
at CPI Group (UK) Ltd
This book is typeset in 10 on 17pt, Dolly Pro.

The paper used in this book comes from the wood pulp of managed forests. For every tree felled, at least one tree is planted, thereby renewing natural resources.

All rights reserved.

No part of this publication may be copied, reproduced or transmitted in any form or by any means without written permission of the publishers.

A CIP catalogue record for this book is available from the British Library.

5 4 3 2 1

In memory of my brother Bartley Higgins,
who died on 16 August 2022.

Loss is the greatest two-timer of all.
It lets on that everything will be grand,
then a wave of grief comes down the road
and flattens you.
– Rita Ann Higgins

In memory of my sister-in-law
Noreina Browne (née Higgins),
who died on 2 December 2023.

CONTENTS

Foreword	1
New Year's Day	5
Epiphany	7
I Thought I Saw Saint Brigid Today	9
Coming Out of Winter	11
Cuckoo	13
The Alphabet of Trees	15
Saint Patrick's Day	17
My Mother Loved Me in Red	19
They Believe in Clint Eastwood	21
April Fool's Day in Jerusalem	23
Primula Vulgaris	25
The Bees Are Coming	27
The Púca	29
Saint Brendan Meets Judas Iscariot	31
Hermit of Glendalough	35
The Eyes Have It	39

Almost Communication	43
He Leaves the Ironing Board Open	45
Whitethorn	47
Lúnasa	49
My Tan, My Tan, My Kingdom for a Tan	53
Edict	57
Fahrenheit	59
I Liked My Father at Halloween	61
This Day I Was Older	63
All Saints' Day	67
All Souls' Day	69
Men with Tired Hair	71
Vortex with a Vision	73
The Valley of Disappointment	75
Pleione	77
Visiting My Father at Christmas	79
Sacred as a Sepulchre	83
Saint Stephen's Day	85
Mummers	89
Healing on the Inside	91
Acknowledgements	93

FOREWORD

'You know, the truth can be really powerful stuff. Because you're not expecting it.'
– Kurt Vonnegut

Like most Irish people, I was educated to a very high standard to believe that poetry was opaque and that mere mortals couldn't understand it on their own. It required interpretation, analysis, critical evaluation, an explanation of the references. The gist of our education is that the poet was trying to say something, but he – it was usually a he – didn't say it very well or very clearly, so he needed help to convey it to the readers. That help was provided by someone called a teacher, who knew what the poems meant, and would try and explain it to us.

We were also led to believe that poetry was nice. It was about nature and clouds and love, and people's better angels and even God.

So I was curious then when Rita Ann came into my life. I liked her, but I wouldn't exactly have called her nice. Her poems weren't nice either. And what's more, I understood them, and they made me feel feelings, without any mediation or interpretation needed.

Years went by, I got a radio show, and the same weekend I started the radio show, the whole country shut down. I'll always remember that first Saturday. I was having some class of a nervous breakdown. But luckily there was a national nervous breakdown going on.

We realised very quickly we needed some poetry. And we remembered Rita Ann. So she somehow became this poetic first responder, capturing the mood, providing solace, putting it in perspective, giving us a laugh at ourselves and always the thorn on the rose, always the fly in the ointment, always the grit in the oyster. Week in, week out, she comforted us, but she never let us get comfortable.

And more importantly, she was a living argument for the fact that poetry was a muscular, solid, useful thing in a crisis.

No one ever really told me poems could be exciting. But in those mad days, when we all looked for our dopamine from a takeaway coffee or a delivery man coming with a package, there was no greater hit than a freshly minted poem dropping into my email inbox, hot off the presses. It was like fresh-baked sourdough. I'd say she was typing them with oven gloves on, they were that hot and fresh.

And I see now too what we demanded of her, and what she demanded of herself. She had to make poetry work as journalism, medicine, religion, solace, stand-up comedy. She had to make it work for 19 year olds and 90 year olds, for the bored, the grieving, the angry, the scared, the hopeless. And she did and they loved it, and they loved her, even though she wasn't always nice. Because they knew she was telling the truth, and she made them laugh, and she made them see things more clearly, with a tiny bit more hope. And so she became the pandemic poet laureate.

She never waved her art or artistry in your face. She never acted the big poet with us, never moaned about muses or moods. Like a real artist, she approached it as an artisan, chipping away every week, revising and improving. No big deal. Just another email: 'I think this is better now'.

And of course, she was just as good outside of that communal baptism of fire. She was doing all that long before then, and she's been doing it since. And she remains the people's poet. An outsider to academia and 'The Awts', Rita Ann is the poetry of the factory floor, of Lanzarote, of the Irish family in all its glorious dysfunction, of neighbours on the road who could be bitches and bolloxes, of the hypocrisy of our betters, of calling out your bullshit and mine.

That this poetry is made by a woman who came late, and from a different angle, to the written word, seems to make it all the more its own.

For me, the best people are the tricky ones, but with the big hearts that would bleed out all over the place if they let them, but they don't let them. Because they have a bit of decorum and mystery for God sake.

Maybe that's what the best poets are too.

Back to Kurt Vonnegut then: 'The function of the artist is to make people like life better than they have before.' And by test, she functions. You'd even say she functions at a high level. Maybe the highest levels.

I hope we appreciate her while she's here. She's magic. She's a one-off. And I'd say she's not too pushed about legacy. Let's read these poems out loud and enjoy them now. And let's tell her she's great while she can enjoy it. She'll bat it away and pretend not to enjoy it. But I'd say she'd go home and tell Christy with a quiet satisfaction.

Brendan O'Connor

NEW YEAR'S DAY

It's New Year's Day,
time for the turkey walk,
and other good intentions.
The turkey walk can be fun
you, walking with other turkeys.
Some walk the turkey off,
some just walk the walk
and talk the turkey talk.

Option two
you could walk on Ballyloughane Beach
as you often do.
You walk to a certain point
and leave your troubles there.
They are invisible
but they can be weighty –
dragging the sap out of your day.

Walking back
from option two
you will feel lighter,
ennui absent.
You will do the same tomorrow

but tomorrow doesn't count.
You only have today,
the day you are in.
Be as odd in it as you will.

Make a place
for that pushy *seanfhocail*,
skirting on the temporal lobe
cluck clucking –
then it lands.
Giorraíonn beirt bóthar.

EPIPHANY

It was the twelfth night,
or small Christmas.
Our mother lit twelve candles,
and you picked one as yours
and whatever candle burnt out first
meant that person would
be the first to die.
We had no sense
and only saw the fun in it.
If your candle blew out
with a draft
it wasn't good either.
Drafts were common in our house
and to the young mind
they held a portent quality
and you might let out
a put-on shiver and say 'Who's there?'
The drafts crept around the gable end
and made the house rattle.
No Christmas candle could survive that.
But there were worse things than drafts
and flickering candles.

That heavy darkness that enveloped
every footfall after Christmas.
It made you long for *coiscéim cearc*.
And you heard it said.
Tá coiscéim cearc ann.
The day is a hen's step longer.

I THOUGHT I SAW SAINT BRIGID TODAY

Pushing a buggy round the estate,
two in the buggy and one on the drag.
As cold as it was out –
she knew inside her house was colder.
She is waiting for the next leckie instalment.
Not due till March.

She did spare it. She bathed the kids less often.
The tumble dryer was always on the blink
it was easier not to use it.
The immersion was the killer.
Where she lives is like Overcoat Drive –
they wear their coats indoors.
They are all Saint Brigids there
in Salt of the Earth Drive.

This woman is kind,
she smiles with her eyes,
a flick of a smile sincerely meant.
She worries about the Communion money
even though it's a long way off.

She knows that if she breaks the Weetabix
and waters down the milk
less will feel like more.
She knows how to make things go further.
Her nerves go further and further.

She walks a tightrope with her budget
that never lasts the week.
By Tuesday the moneylenders are lurking.
Their code is nod and grin.
The nod means nothing –
but she knows how to interpret the grin –
the moneylender's grin.

COMING OUT OF WINTER

He wanted to sack the organist.
Not because she'd burst into
her own rendition of
'Under the Boardwalk'
at an ill-suited time.

The main problem he had with her
was her saying February
was the start of spring,
and she said it non-stop
on Saint Brigid's Day.

The organist
a word-sparer by nature,
could wallop up
a nasty turn of phrase
that would rip the calcium
out of your bones
if you percolated her space.

The maestro listened to his bones
and his bones said, we are still in winter.
He threw a gimlet eye on the organist

as she pottered round town
saying out-of-season stuff.

Some say there was a chemistry between them.

February could be a poisonous month
as far as the Siberian wind chill went.
Her talk of spring was benign,
she used it out of a kind of craving
not even she understood.

He just hated out-of-season stuff.
She wanted to put
the long days of winter behind her.

If I were him, a local seer said,
I would not sack the organist.
In fact, I would give her a raise
and a new car, a blue Chevrolet.

Once after a cake sale
to help put a new roof on the local chapel
the organist was overheard saying,
'If I won the pools I'd buy myself
a blue Chevrolet and drive it
all the way to Monaghan,
on the first of February every year.'

CUCKOO

The cuckoo lays eggs in other bird's nests,
making a right fool out of the meadow pipit,
the reed warblers.
They will rear the cuckoo's young,
while *mo dhuine* flies off Scott free.

Cuculus Canorus,
harbinger of summertime
plucker of morsels, gauger of time.
We learn from the cuckoo-taggers,
that his winter habitat is no longer a secret.
He covered nine thousand kilometres,
two continents, several countries.
How long is a piece of string?

Cuach KP's tracker tells us
KP spent the winter in the Congo
where he fattens himself up.
He flew on from the Bay of Biscay
to the kingdom of Kerry.

No one knows what kept Cuculus Canorus rapt
on his long sea journey to his Irish habitat,

the disappearing habitat, the pest of pesticides.
Maybe thoughts of a hairy caterpillar
with snails and insects on the side! Who knows?

The cuckoo's salacious reputation is gone
like the scorched hedgerow.
He's now the king, the undisputed king.
He's King of the piece of string.

THE ALPHABET OF TREES

I don't think
that they met.
In fact I'm nearly
sure they didn't.
At least he never met her,
he met a different her
she met a different him.

Those surrogates
were wearing the threads of others
speaking the lingo
of dishcloth and discontent,
cloning their idiosyncrasies,
the liberty of it.
It wasn't him –
she wasn't there either.
They looked for signs of themselves
in these imposters.

It was strange for them
seeing the doppelgängers
walking down the street.
They could have been Beatrice and Benedict.

Smart an-all as the Gods were,
they got his height wrong,
they made him smaller,
they put a few extra pounds on her hips.
She raised an eyebrow
at some lesser deity sending out
those construction workers
to build a moat around his word house,
enough full stops to choke an ass.

No pasarán drifting in and out
of the stucco in hieroglyphic symbols.
Not a good idea to *no pasarán* her
while you're wearing
someone else's walk,
it won't wash.
Not when it is written
in the Alphabet of Trees –
that if they kiss,
they'll end in smithereens.

SAINT PATRICK'S DAY

I was earwigging –
for the said and the unsaid,
for the badge, for the buttonhole,
for the glossy, for the green.

I skipped to a neighbour's house –
I had tales to tell.
We weren't getting any
badges and green ribbons
on this Saint Patrick's Day.
I might have used the
'can't afford' words –
Whatever words I used
were the wrong words.
The response was calamitous.

You let the family down.
You brought shame, a sea of shame.
As God is my judge
you will go back and reverse all this.
You will undo the hurt you have caused.
You will skip back and tell the neighbour
that we are falling down with

green badges and ribbons.
Our thoughts are green.
Our prayers are green.
Our hens are green.

You will come back and close the gate
and accept the rebuke;
you overheard wrong
you misunderstood
and in future my girl,
when adults are talking
you will listen less
for things that were never said.

Now hop it with your pig-tales,
your tall-tales, tales that don't always
stand up to scrutiny.
Tales that take the scenic route;
the high road
the green road
the road to no-town.

MY MOTHER LOVED ME IN RED

I saw my mother's grave
from the top of the bus recently.
She died in 1971
I only saw her grave
from this angle a few days ago.

I was a great one for the buses years ago.
I even wrote a poem about it.
Then we got the Arts Council bursary car
and that was the end of the buses for me.

Now that I have the bus pass –
I'd be inclined to use the bus more often –
plus, I can see my mother's grave
from the upper deck.

I say nothing to the other passengers
as we pass the graveyard.
Much as I want to shout –
Inside that wall,
four graves in to the left
lies a good woman –
Margaret Mary Higgins,

who died aged fifty-five.
She gave birth to twelve –
one died at six months.
Joachim Mary had a hole in his heart.

My mother loved me in red,
she would say,
'Red is lovely on you'
she told me this, not often
but as often as she could –
while the other ten were out of earshot –
which in truth was as likely;
as a lunar eclipse,
a ghost rainbow,
or meeting a natterjack on the run.

THEY BELIEVE IN CLINT EASTWOOD

In Cork prison
on Ash Wednesday
the warders have
black crosses painted
where the Cyclops
had his eye.

They believe in
the Trinity,

They believe in
reincarnation,

They believe in
dust and ashes,

They believe in
Jesus with long hair,

They believe in
Clint Eastwood,

They believe in
key consortium;

They believe in
the letter of the law.

APRIL FOOL'S DAY IN JERUSALEM

The soldiers were everywhere –
running up and down steps,
in and out of this street,
this way that way zigzag way
around corners in their twenties.

I asked what was going on.
It's nothing, the man said,
they have to circumnavigate
and go through the streets,
and go through the houses,
they zigzag a little,
they up and down a little,
they around corners a lot,
it's nothing, enjoy the sunshine.

PRIMULA VULGARIS

In May the statue of Our Lady
was cleaned and put out
in a sheltered place in the garden.
A lick of blue paint took years off her,
we dolled her up further with bouquets of mayflowers.
We'd put a string of primroses around her neck
and another one above the front door.
The fairies would never pass
over or under a primrose string.

Yesterday when I was leaving Annegret's
for a walk down to the shore,
the primroses were out to play.
As I walked they seemed to walk.
Some decked a hedgerow,
other clusters claimed a field.
How could they be *vulgaris* anything?

We'd put fresh flowers
around Our Lady's statue.
She was a good protector
against the dark forces.

We had to be on our guard,
our side eye never closed.
Demons hid under every cowslip.

As for the fairies,
they had no dark side,
only mischief-makers in the main.
They might toss a bucket in the air
or move a spade that was left against a wall.
Or so we thought. Did you see that spade move?
Who tossed that bucket in the air?
'Puck did,' was the only reply.

On my way back to the house
the primroses were there again,
more plentiful than before.
Who sprayed that hill?
Who knitted that hedgerow?
I walk through a funnel of colour,
a pale-yellow dress,
not a fairy in sight.
Sabhaircín sabhaircín.

THE BEES ARE COMING

Didn't we miss
lots of seasons that time.
Wasn't it mostly dark and darker?
The sameness of things was hard to stomach.

Snowdrops, daffodils and crocuses
gave us colder days,
but we loved their coats and colours.

Now you notice the morning light
getting earlier and earlier.
The birdsong is welcome,
you nearly hold your breath to listen,
you never knew nature
and the seasons meant so much.

The buds are peeping
and popping.
Cherry blossom with its pink gush and blush
is ahead of you on all journeys –
pick-ups and drop-offs
walks to the local beach.

The tadpoles are busy.
The caterpillar move is slow
but it is on,
entire families of them.

The bees are coming
looking for nectar.
We are nicer
looking for nectar too.
We are smiling –
hope is hanging around
seedlings are sprouting
spring is here.

THE PÚCA

I asked my mother if it was a sign
of something that my Communion veil
was sticking to Judy Connor's at the altar.

Herself and Mrs Burke with their arms folded
under their big cushioned breasts
were giving harum-scarum glances and *mar-Dhea* sighs.
They were at the start of a laughing session
that would end with tears being wiped away
by the tail end of their flowery aprons.

And why wouldn't it be a sign
didn't my mother and her sisters in from Maree
talk in signs and *piseogs* all the time?
Every rickety move any Ballybrit bird made
was a sign of something or other.
Jackdaw, crow, magpie or maggot.

And if the goats shat on your dahlias,
God knows who was going to get an airmail letter
full to the brink with bad vowels and bile.
'God bless the mark', was used for everything, not just
when your neighbour's child had a strawberry birthmark

on their eyelid as big and bright as a peony rose.
And if anyone heard the Banshee's cry
that was it, some poor devil was a gonner.

Our days were one long *piseog*
and the Púca was there too to frighten the wits out of us.
It was the Púca you would meet in all his malevolence
when you found yourself at the bottom of the well
if you dared poke your snout out after dark.

But good God, who never slept
was always flung like holy water
during a thunderstorm, between you and all harm,
and the Púca, like the cuckoo, could go and spit.

SAINT BRENDAN MEETS JUDAS ISCARIOT

When Brendan was off with the monks
searching for the Promised Land,
he took a sharp left
at that eerie mountain
where demons ducked and dived
and grabbed one of his men.
That turned out to be –
the entrance to hell.
The jagged rock is above water
and known to some as Rockall.

If you see a wretched-looking man,
with cuts all over his face,
pinned on that rock in the middle
of an angry body of water –
you won't immediately know
that he is Judas Iscariot.
The bleeding face and eyes make
him look more like a mythological creature
up from the deep.

The cloak is hung on two iron forks.
With the help of the lashing winds,
the cloak is walloping Judas
across the face and eyes –
taking strips out of him.

Saint Brendan asks how could anyone
deserve such a punishment?
This is no punishment, says Judas,
I am the worm who betrayed Jesus,
and for what, thirty pieces of silver!
There are places in this world where
no amount of silver can help you.

This is a respite from hell
compared to my usual day.
I get respite from the flames on Sundays
and on other holy days.
Being stuck here on this rock
is the good that happens in my life,
compared to the other –
when the demons drag me back there.

Judas said to Brendan,
You know that place of abject misery
where one of your men
was dragged kicking and screaming –

that is the mouth of hell.
That is where I generally reside.

Brendan asks Judas
where the whipping cloak came from,
and Judas told him,
that he had given it to a leper
to shield him from the heat of the sun.
It turns out that Judas had
stolen the cape first.

He volunteered to Brendan
other good deeds he had done.
But the demons, who always had a full ear
weren't having a bar of it –
and when Judas slept
for five consecutive seconds
they wrenched him back to hell
for a right roasting, and the rest.

Judas was grateful for the mercy days
when he could get them.
His emptiness was complete.
After all he was forever
in the in-between place –
where you felt but didn't feel,
where you heard but didn't hear.

Where you saw but didn't see.
He was for all eternity –
lodged between hell and high water.

HERMIT OF GLENDALOUGH
FOR LILIAN DALTON

Saint Kevin of Glendalough
in all his quietness and solemnity,
never thought of himself as holy.
His love of words and prayer,
were always for others,
his 'self' didn't exist.

When he was younger
he could carry fire close to his chest,
it would neither burn nor scar.
Older Kevin would recite psalms
from the holy book,
in the freezing stream of goodwill.
One day he lost the book of prayer.

An otter retrieved it
and proffered it up
on the tip of its snout –
in pristine condition, and dry.
The same otter caught
salmon for him and all in his monastery.
The otter had small ears and good hearing.

When a monk suggested the otter's pelt
would make smashing gloves
to help banish their chilblains,
the otter scarpered.

Stories travelled,
about how close to nature Kevin was,
about the white cow, the giving cow.
The sheep that were gone but not gone,
the blackbird was famous.

When the wild boar
was being hunted
by man and hounds,
they came across Kevin
on his knees in prayer,
birds perched on his shoulders.
The hounds lay down in a docile stretch.
The boar ran free.

Kevin the Hermit.
Ascetic of Glendalough –
renewed in prayer.
His internal barometer
only clocking up calm.

A bed of stone,
a pillow of rock
a prayer for every living thing.
A word without malice,
Amen.

THE EYES HAVE IT

These two, sitting halfway down the plane.
Howard Hughes nails,
eyelashes long enough to sweep
the length of Skeheenarinky.
Miniest of denim skirts,
legs long and identical.
Fake tan streaks
in exactly the same place –
the cracks of the knees.

The two wans
lose empty bottles
down the side of their seats.
Miniature in-flight
Grey Goose vodka bottles.
They asked for grey duck,
the flight attendant
knew what they meant.
One says, it was definitely a duck or a drake
and it was flying in my direction.
They squash the tonic cans in unison,
they laugh while their bodies heave.

Their lives
are a sliding scale of;
plonk plonk – scream
squash the tonic-can dream.
Grey duck grey goose on the loose.
How much I want to be them?

The pilot
tells us we'll soon
be flying over Fatima.
With this the two are in convulsions.
Your young wan, one says.
I know, the other says –
reading her best friend's mind.

She calls me Fatty-Ma
she says Fatty-Ma have you seen
me-eyelashes, the waterproofs
with a side serving of glue.
They're called Envy Eyes,
AKA the demi-wispies,
with the doe glow ...
They last from seven to ten days
if ya don't blink.
They got mileage out
out of their own gags,
and how they howled!

And you say,
eyelashes, eyelashes,
where would I be going
with fake eyelashes,
and my eyes as small
as Tubbercurry sloes?
And they laugh some more.

ALMOST COMMUNICATION

My father just passed me
in his Fiat 127
I was cycling my bicycle 'Hideous'.

They stopped at O'Meara's
for the *Connacht Tribune*.
As I passed I shouted
'Road hog' in the window.

The occupants laughed.

Before this he owned
a Renault 12,
we called it
the 'Ballyhaunis Cow Killer'.

Later we met outside the sister's,
'Wouldn't you think
he'd buy you a decent bike, the miser.'

'If he had your money,' I said
and we laughed.

The neighbours with their ears
to the rose bushes
think that we're great friends.

I haven't seen his eyes for years.

HE LEAVES THE IRONING BOARD OPEN

He likes
crisp white shirts
and Tracey Chapman.
He leaves
the ironing-board open
in his mobile home
near the motorway,
so that he is halfway there
if he ever makes the decision
to go out.

He plays
Tracey Chapman
really loud
in his mobile home
near the motorway,
so that he can't hear
the noise of the cars
or the screech of his loneliness
crashing into him
from every side.

WHITETHORN

Whitethorn is nearly covering Tuar Beag,
a christening blanket with thorns.
When I see it I think of my mother's warning.

'Don't ever bring whitethorn into the house
for fear it would bring the *mí-ádh* upon us
and attach itself to one of the youngsters
not yet walking but carrying their dividends of venial sin.'

(Do ye renounce Satan? We do)

The force, with no name or place in this dimension
might drag one of them angels down with the fever
or some fierce shaking calamity.

Unseen with the naked eye
the force could take one half of the twins
down to the fairy fort or further
into the fog in Coyne's field, never to be seen again.

'The lord protect us from all harm,
don't ever bring that whitethorn into the house.'

(Do ye renounce Satan? We do.)

LÚNASA

We celebrate Lugh the Celtic God.
He could bring a good harvest or a bad storm
depending on the flap he was in.
Sure aren't we all Celts to our pelts nowadays.
You'd hear them say it at the bus stop.
How's your mother? She's a right Celt
since she got the bunions,
after traipsing around town
in them paper shoes.
We know Lúnasa is a time for rituals,
let us let autumn in, the first harvest,
let us give and keep giving.
Let us celebrate abundance
in all its guises.

Slush puppies and invoices.
Consultancy fees, fi's, fo's and fums.
First fruits, ritual flip-flop play.
The barter fund was funnelling,
someone else was tunnelling,
for bilberries, for blackberries,
for blueberries for gooseberries.
Flip it, flop it, just don't drop it.

Part of the pagan tradition was
to gift the less fortunate
easy-peeler shoes, slip-in-and-slip-out shoes
guilt free flops that you can wear on
'See No Evil Street'.

Lúnasa a time of abundance
A time for collecting –
get your television licence,
its two-for-one Monday –
A time for giving, get a cab.
A falling from grace, not a trace.
If only they had asked us.
Take that, take the other, take a pay cut.
Never be sullied, bullied or Killinaskullied.
The fog, the bog, the putrid air.
We were glued to our television sets.
We didn't gloat, we just gagged at the flip-flop jokes
that were tumbling out, in pre-Lúnasa abundance.
How many flip-flops does it take
to walk a catawampus mile?
It's Lúnasa, a time for renewals
a time for dancing and prancing.
A time to fill your baskets –
fill your pockets while you're at it.
Is everything clear now?
I want to say yes, but I'd be lying.

Nothing is clear while the ear worm
loops around your noggin
like a dervish asking,
'What makes the world go round
the world go round, the world go round?'

MY TAN, MY TAN, MY KINGDOM FOR A TAN

I'm not going back to that school,
when I say the teacher hates me
you'll say he does not
and why don't we go and pick out
a lovely new school bag, as if I was eight.

I don't want to go back to school
you think a new school bag
is the 'Be all and end all'.

You'll say, *that quote comes when Macbeth*
is thinking of murdering King Duncan
You are learning a lot at that school my son.

I'm not going back to that school
I'll be meeting people I haven't seen for ages,
have you any idea how difficult that is
I've changed over the summer
people will laugh at me.
At my spots.
You'll say, *everyone gets spots.*

None of my class on INSTA have spots
But INSTA makes the world spot free you'll say,
your friends might have other things that bother them.
And you'll list off – weight gain, acne and much more.

I don't know what kind of a parent you think you are,
saying my friends have weight issues
and are covered in this and covered in that.
I'm the one who is covered from head to toe
in that ugly uniform.
The trousers feel like they are spun from bull wire and thorn
and the jumper is the most dated green I've ever seen,
should be unseen like the poetry they make us learn.

And another thing,
if I am going back to that school
which is highly unlikely
that lunchbox has to go
I'm sick of all that You stuff –
quinoa like jaded frogspawn
I am not eating that.
I want a wrap or a supermarket bap
I want crisps and a fizzy and pot noodles.

And you know the worst thing,
worse than the quinoa,

worse than the
sight-unseen yesterday's green
dyed-in-the-wool jumper –
my tan my lovely tan
is covered from head to toe
and back to spleen,
my tan I worked so diligently on,
is never going to be seen.
My tan, my tan, my kingdom for a tan.

EDICT

Go to Tuar Beag and sing for her.
Take only left turns
pass out the whitethorn
but remember to pay homage,
admire it as it should be admired
pay no heed to the *piseog* brigade.

Stay with her *lon dubh*, perch and be ready.
Watch out for straws in the wind
eggshells, a lone magpie
a wendy goat, mistletoe out of season.

Keep an eye on Regret
jaywalker by day, shape-shifter by chance
and Despair, a weasel waiting to lunge.
Settle and sing, blackbird, sleep not.

FAHRENHEIT

A cloud drapes itself over Tuar Beag
nearly sending me under the table.

Last night the clocks went back an hour.
I say obvious things like
it will soon be dark at four
and other mundanes.
We can hardly walk the bog now.

I feel like Iris of the Lost Rainbow
spoiling for a storm.
I can hear you shouting at the horses on TV
you don't hear what I'm saying
but you reply anyway,
'Yeah it was a rotten year for blackberries.'

When the summoned gusts
blow down the *bóithrin*
and rip the buttons off your shirt
you'll care then,
your widescreen in the ditch.

Aeolus comes without *plámás*
loyal wind bag that he is.
The squall gains strength,
galvanised roofs, loose teeth
chattering jaw joints
ice sheets and whirlwind,
a Connemara cyclone.

I LIKED MY FATHER AT HALLOWEEN

It gets earlier every year.
The bangers start going off
when October isn't even
a shadow in the hall.

Nothing much happens when the zombies
and witches statue at your door.
They hold wide open
the plunder bag and you throw the booty in.
They rarely raise a rhyme, a skipping song,
or half a random rattle-tattle,
tic-tac-two song,
much less a *'Halloween is coming.'*

I liked my father at Halloween.
He got into the swing of things.
When we tried to bite the apples
that were hanging from the door hinge
on coil-around twine,
peals of laughter echoed off the walls.
We became the whirling dervish,
our hands secured behind our backs.
Nose-butting the apples every time.

When we tried to get
that threepenny bit or a tanner
out of the basin of water with our teeth –
his giant's laughter filled the house again.

No need to hedge our bets
when it came to the *bairin breac* –
fever pitch was nothing
as we watched out for that ring,
monkey nuts were flush and teeming.

You feel for the cats and dogs
who are terrified
of the bangers going off.
You pity yourself
for harbouring memories
that tightrope the threshold
of melancholy.
You pity the children
who know no rhymes.

THIS DAY I WAS OLDER

Pain on wakening, my shoulders, down my legs.
This day I was older. I reached for my phone.
Pain was a fat ten, I took my hand back.
Phones are overrated.
Washing my hair – pain was a twelve
hair-washing was overrated.
Then the bra straps – yada yada,
bras are overrated.

In no time
I was a scruffy braless crank
with PMR to my name.
Old age was snapping,
then along came steroids
and I didn't need a broom.
I was always hungry.
Things that shouldn't go went –
caramelised onion and sweet cake.

Eighteen months the steroids sentence, enough
time to strip the goodness from your bones,
We'll taper you off them when the time comes.
I don't think you really 'have it' the man says.

I tapered down and down the rabbit hole of clinic visits.
Then one day I was tapered.
You are now a tapered woman
and there is nowhere to hide.

Time was no healer,
it passed me like a raging train
on the brink of an assault.
Old killjoy inflammation
came back and landed on my love handles
making me walk funny.

My gait was no longer mine.
I couldn't pick me out of a walking line-up
if I had to walk that line.
Bursitis, the man says,
the man always knows.

Try aqua aerobics, try a foam roller
walk further, do it faster.
Never turn around, keep your beak facing north.
Nowadays I surf around the landing
on my foam roller, never naked it must be said.
Sometimes I wear an old leather pants –
just for pig iron.

I'm afraid of the aqua aerobics group
I see them in the pool
they will devour me. I will sink.
The walking I can do
with someone else's walk.
I never go anywhere
without my Free Travel Pass.
I walk so far then I hop on a bus,
maybe hop is a bit of a boast –

I get to there and I'll walk
most of the way home.
Anything to be carried has to go on my back
I wear a small haversack – the pilgrims' progress.
Sometimes my shoulders act the maggot
but never on feast days or holy days of subjugation.

Currently, I have a solitary gallstone
as big as mortal sin otherwise
my gallbladder is unremarkable.
That has to come out, the man says.
Until then, I foam roll on the landing
I walk faster and further
I never look back.

ALL SAINTS' DAY

The day before All Souls'.
It was an easier day.
You could rattle them off,
Saint Martin, Saint Rita,
Saint Jude, patron saint of lost causes.
Saint Anthony, pray to him
when you lost your shoe,
and it would appear.
Abracadabra.

We called up
all the saints we knew,
and asked their intersession.
None of us knew what it meant.
It was said Saint Anthony was good
for the lost keys as well.
We knew nothing of keys,
there were no walls or fences.
All freedom was ours
except our thought,
that was harnessed by the church.

Saint Rita and the bees,
oh the bees and the baptism.
The bees entered Saint Rita's mouth
and out they swarmed causing her no harm.
She is worth something,
there is a rose called after her.
She is worth a Hail Mary,
She is worth a lost shoe.

ALL SOULS' DAY

Novembers were dark
and the responsibility was great.
You had to get the souls out of Purgatory.

Write their names down,
no matter how distant a relative
they were.

Be sure and place the list
in the altar-cavity,
where Gods' messenger on Earth
would find it.
He loved a game of hide and seek.

Always be afraid,
have guilt and shame
in equal measure.
Don't forget to pray and pray.
You have a responsibility
to the souls in Purgatory.

You are eight –
don't let others
sense your fear.

Pray more,
don't leave anyone
caught in the flames.

MEN WITH TIRED HAIR

On a bank holiday Monday in Galway,
you can see old men
sitting on window sills in Prospect Hill.

Time is not a factor here,
only images pleasing and displeasing
to the men with tired hair.

Despite this easiness with life,
there is a waiting, a look out
in anticipation of something.

The looking up and down continues;
the awaited stimulus always comes.

Days, it's a young woman.
Streets, it's a fire.
Years, it's news of a tragedy in far off Dublin.

VORTEX WITH A VISION

The inflammation
took up squatter's rights.
The right hand wouldn't write.
Writing with the left hand was new,
it quietened the mind, a balm.
Serene and hopeful. Who is this person?

I liked the one writing with her left hand
she was me but I didn't know her name.
She was chilled, she laughed more.
Her left-handed alphabet was obelisk-straight.
The latter-day *citóg* didn't concern herself
with other people's wars, the news could wait.
Things could slip. Disasters could slide.
Slender L's and K's beckoned the other letters,
an alphabet dance, a siege of synonyms.
Vowels no longer vicious,
The ampersand was a two-hand reel.

The right-handed Kraken was stirring.
The one who bristled and hissed as the world was let in.
Reaching out for her glasses, her phone, the day's bad news,
a rogue current burning the nerve endings.

I'm pain and I'm pleased to meet you.
Bone density, Dexa scan, injection man.

With some luck she will taper down
the steroid shaft.
A vortex with a vision,
next thing you know –
she'll be reading the Bible.

THE VALLEY OF DISAPPOINTMENT

The treachery of expectations
will catch you every time
and lead you into the valley of disappointment,
and further into a field of scorched grass.

The valley of disappointment is deep
it starts and ends with time-old treachery.
You walk in like Isaac Van Amburgh
and you walk out like a Tessie the Turtle,
humble as a back rasher
and just as flat.

The contract never tells you
the steamroller has your face on it,
with every purple spider vein highlighted.
No, the contract only says,
me love you long time
dance monkey dance.

The valley of disappointment is deep
it goes down to the centre of the earth.
Just because you have magpie genes

doesn't mean you have to always
follow the bauble.

Expectations, second cousin of treachery
never times removed.
Trinkets bring you up, reality brings you down.
Expectation is the corner boy here
catching your eye, giving you the *come hither*
it means nothing.
Only a jaded flirt would fall for it.

You were fodder for the clapboard
and the claptrap.
What now for the internal warp
that's dragging you all over the shop.
It was never about you, you poor eejit.
So, stop crying at the bus stop and move on.

PLEIONE

Pleione will give you
all the time you need,
if only you could find her.

She's more sea-nymph than anything
she'd tell you herself, but where is she?
She minded the flocks too –
that's how she got her name.

You can roam around all day
calling her name,
she'll grant you that indulgence.
Be careful never to call her Little Bo-Peep,
she hates lame humour.
People call their yachts after her –
they could do less.

You could have sworn
you caught a glimpse of her
at the Maxol garage
filling up the SUV.
It will never be her
she will have left long ago
for the last comet home.

Orion looked for her for seven years
and couldn't find her.
This was before he stepped on a scorpion.
The poor Amadán never heard
of the eggshell approach.

Pleione's daughters were sick with grief.
Zeus took pity on them and turned all seven into stars.
Look up. While the Pleiades shimmer –
they don't always shine.

VISITING MY FATHER AT CHRISTMAS

How hard could it be?
Duck in, a bit of small talk
duck out, dodging the bullets
and fire a few myself,
how hard could it be?

The booby traps are under
the Quality Street box.
Tread softly, start again,
it will be easy
a piece of cake,
dyspepsia maybe
or no heart scald at all.

A short journey
or a long haul,
the choice is mine.
Watch out for black ice,
by nature sly
by day a looking glass.

There are no footpaths
no kerbs to fall off

this territory is wide open
a plate underfoot.

Words matter
words don't matter
speak when you're spoken to.
Spokes are a snare
silence is the hardest station.
Remember the fifth commandment.

Plenty to talk about
the frost, the treachery of ice
the black ice.

The heat of the room
the great fire,
that's a great fire
the Quality Street
and who brought them.
The new couch and chairs.
That's a lovely couch, is it new?
The great fire,
we did the fire already,
next get-out clause where are you?

The television,
same bloody programmes every year.

That television is going back.
The turkey, yeah the turkey,
tough as the sole of my shoe
mind you the stuffing was champion
the ham, yeah the ham
a pillar of salt.

Then the more mundane.
Do you know anything
that will get rid of heartburn?
Snakes and bladders.

Then down to the knitty bitty,
he was working up to it
lifting the head as if to say something
then saying nothing.
Silence is a tough station.

I had that heartburn
two years ago when you called as well.
Where did you get that *cape outa*?
Strange-looking yoke for a girl to be wearing.
Is it second-hand?
People wear anything nowadays
any old rag at all,
it looks like a shroud.
'It would look good on you then.'

You were sharpening your tongue
for a week for that one, he'd say.
I'll bet you don't know the Irish for shroud though!

The years between us
ticked and tocked, snaked and bladdered
down the whole gastric-acid afternoon.
The Christmas tree glistening
the talking clock saying nothing,
not a hiccup at all.

SACRED AS A SEPULCHRE

That Christmas
the lone phone box
at the centre of things
was hopping.
The word got out
that the calls were free.
People came from four directions
out of their council houses
to speak to loved ones
as far away as Canada
and New Zealand.
Most people rang Boston.
The queue was snaking
round the avenues.
Cigarettes were shared
with people you would hardly speak to
during the year.
Someone had silver mints.
Whispering Missus Coyle had Zubes.
One man, forever nicknamed
the shop steward,
told people not to stay on too long

in case someone
at the telephone exchange copped it.
The back-and-forth conversations
interconnecting these random lives
were precious and free,
and less random than you'd think.
Melancholy and laughter skipped the queue.
Sometimes melancholy won.
Back then to sensible talk, like,
what time is it there?
And, what's the weather like,
it's raining here.
The phone box with its one hinge missing
was now as sacred as a sepulchre,
a keeper of secrets
a place for weather reports
a melancholy barometer
a place for missing beats.

SAINT STEPHEN'S DAY

There was always frost,
and twigs crunched underfoot
and the tip of your nose
felt like it would fall off.
You could hear cap guns
going snap, snap, snap.
It was that time of year
and the girls got dolls
that broke easily,
soon enough you would see
a skinny doll's limb
or a dolls' head on the ground.

Christmas Day was over
and it was time to bury the wren.
The little bird was enticed
into the wooden made trap.
A crumb here and here and here –
and he was inside the cage.
The string was pulled and the
secure trap gate came down.

He was fed more crumbs and water,
not necessarily his last supper.
He looked giddy with us all gazing
in at him. He seemed to always be a him.
No one ever said of the wren,
Isn't she lovely.

I don't recall a dead wren.
The wren boys went door to door
with himself in the cage
hopping with anxiety.

They belted out
The wran the wran the king of all birds
Saint Stephens' Day was caught in the furze ...
Up with the kettles and down with the pans
Give us a penny to bury the wran.
Coppers were given
and the wren boys moved on.

In that time and since
a few wrens were caught
and caged, snagged and bagged.
The cap guns were becoming
a thing of the past.

The dolls became more sturdy.
They could stand up for themselves.
They didn't break on Saint Stephen's Day
or the day after or the day after that.

MUMMERS
IN MEMORY OF PADDY MOLONEY

Grown men in women's clothes
they knock so loud,
to wake the dead.
Old rags, their mother's hats
lipstick outside the pale
blood red and gaudy.
Grins smeared to make us laugh,
we laughed and clapped.

We knew them by their 'neighbour's eyes'
we guessed the rest.
Tonight they would dress up
tonight we would go wild.

They hup-hupped, and used half-pagan shouts
half-words were less and howls were more,
bodhrán banter, tin whistle,
one with a handmade drum.
Faces painted orange and red,
one with tinsel behind his ear,
one with long blonde hair.
We knew them by their 'neighbour's eyes'
dresses and tights, half man, high heel, a hairy shin,

tin cans rattled hallelujah.
The squeeze box begged for mercy
whine, wheeze, gasp, yelp,
the bodhrán hammered time.

The tin whistle whistled, it also pined,
like us who knew, it knew too,
the mummers will soon be gone.
Heathens, infidels, idolaters
they banish the goblin
they praise the goat.
They imp, they gimp, they groan
they dance on the spot
a crazy jig, a turkey tune.

The shouts not mortal, the night not real
spoons rasp hard on a mummer's knee.
The melodeon acting like a frantic bull
not asking you to hold your breath,
just never leave space for a lull.

We knew them by their 'neighbour's eyes'
we guessed the rest.
Half-words were less and howls were more
spoons, bodhrán, their tin-can rattle
Saint Stephen's night they would dress up,
Saint Stephen's night we would go wild.

HEALING ON THE INSIDE

When I tell people
the surgery is over
and I'm feeling great,
they say, but don't forget,
You're healing on the inside.
They had to cut through
three layers of gristle
to yank out that gallstone.
Remember that.

We are all healing on the inside,
it doesn't take a gone-off gallstone to
remind us of that.
We have a lot to heal from,
it's not just the triple lock
the Tánaiste talks about.
It's the housing crisis
it's the overcrowding in hospitals
it's the war in Ukraine
The unfair deals
The ubiquitous schemes.

It may come out through a keyhole
but for it to get there takes some journeying.
From the Blue Bayou to Bundoran
from Clare to here.
Give them an Inch and they'll
count heads on the bus.

Sometimes it's too late for the triple lock
It's lost in the manshed at the end of the garden.
Tinkering with a Joe Soap lock is one thing.
Tinkering with a triple lock
is another bag-a-hammers.
We are all healing on the inside
aren't people saying it to me every day of the week.
They lard it over me. The people know.

ACKNOWLEDGEMENTS

Many of these poems were broadcast on *The Brendan O'Connor Show*, RTÉ Radio 1. Some of the poems were broadcast on *Sunday Miscellany*. Some of these poems were broadcast on *Arena*, RTÉ Radio 1.

Some of these poems first appeared in *Ireland is Changing Mother*, published by Bloodaxe Books (2011). 'This day I Was Older' was published in *Well, You Don't Look It! Women Writers in Ireland Reflect on Ageing*, edited by Éilis Ní Dhuibhne and Michaela Schrage-Früh, published by Salmon Publishing (2024). 'Men With Tired Hair' was also published by Salmon, and appears on a plaque located at No 1 Eyre Square, Galway.

Every encounter with the Gill Team was pleasant and professional. I would like to thank all the people I worked with there for their constant help and enthusiasm, for their cheerfulness.

I would like thank Elaine Feeney for her never-ending unconditional support. Brendan O'Connor brought my work to a wider audience, and I will always be grateful to him for this and his steadfast support. I would like to thank Susannah Dickey for her generosity.

To my husband Christy, I say thank you for hanging in there with me all these years. I thank my daughters, Heather and Jennifer, and my grandsons Oisin, Cooper, Axel and Jackson. I say to you all, thank you for always being in my corner. I thank Heather's partner Dermot, who is now part of our gang.

PERMISSIONS

The publishers gratefully acknowledge permission to reprint copyright material in this book as follows:

'Almost Communication', 'April Fool's Day in Jerusalem', 'They Believe in Clint Eastwood' from *Throw in The Vowels: New & Selected Poems* (Bloodaxe Books, 2005), reproduced with permission of Bloodaxe Books.

'Edict', 'Fahrenheit', 'The Púca', 'Visiting My Father At Christmas', 'Whitethorn' from *Ireland is Changing Mother* (Bloodaxe Books, 2011), reproduced with permission of Bloodaxe Books.

'Men With Tired Hair' from *Witch in the Bushes* (Salmon Publishing, 1988), reproduced with permission of Salmon Publishing.

'Primula Vulgaris' from *Tongulish* (Bloodaxe Books, 2016), reproduced with permission of Bloodaxe Books.

'This Day I Was Older' from *Well, You Don't Look It! Women Writers in Ireland Reflect on Ageing* edited by Éilís Ní Dhuibhne and Michaela Schrage-Früh (Salmon Publishing, 2024), reproduced with permission of Salmon Publishing.